A start me up Book

Whales
and Dolphins

By Petra Deimer
Illustrated by Manfred Kostka and Frank Kliemt

*In the ancient Mediterranean dolphins were revered
as intelligent animals. This coin shows a young
man riding on a dolphin.*

Tessloff Publishing

Preface

Human beings have driven whales to the brink of extinction. For a few decades now, however, nature conservationists and animal lovers throughout the world have been working hard to make people aware of the fate these animals are facing. They are doing everything they can to save the whales.

Whales are among the largest creatures that ever existed. They evolved from land mammals but have adapted themselves wonderfully to life in water. Some of them can dive to great depths and for long periods of time. In terms of distance, they migrate farther than any other mammal, finding their way by means of a complex echolocation system. With their sophisticated "songs" they can also communicate with each other over hundreds of miles. They help injured or sick members of their species and they are playful and intelligent, as their performances at large aquariums show. There are many stories about dolphins—a small species within the large whale group—helping people in danger. We have done a poor job repaying them for this help. For centuries whalers have hunted these giants into the farthest corners of the Arctic oceans, harpooned them, and carved them up for their meat and oil. Year after year tens of thousands of whales died, so that some species are now extinct, and most of the other species are very rare. In the past few years we finally passed international laws to protect these huge sea animals. This volume of the **start me up!**™ series provides an overview of the anatomy and behavior of whales. It examines the ways they have been and still are hunted, and it discusses efforts in recent years to protect them.

We hope that humankind will succeed in saving the whale, but sadly we know far too little about the habits of these fascinating, intelligent animals. A large field of research is opening up for behavioral scientists and biologists interested in whales and dolphins.

Volume 5

PUBLISHERS: Tessloff Publishing, Quadrillion Media LLC

EDITOR: Alan Swensen

PICTURE SOURCES: Bildarchiv Preussischer Kulturbesitz, Berlin: pp. 36b, 40, 41; Archiv Deimer/IFAW: pp. 12, 13, 19, 24, 36 ca, 47; Archiv Deimer/François Gohier: pp. 17b, 35; Archiv Deimer/Schomer: pp. 42 tl, 42b; Archiv Deimer/Schreiber: pp. 12, 42 tc; Deimer, Hamburg: pp. 7, 39l, 39b, 42tr, 43t (3), 43b, 44, 45 (2), 46 (2), 48; dpa: p. 38b; Graner/GSM: p. 10; Kiefner: p. 6; Okapia, Frankfurt: pp. 26, 27, 31, 38t, 39tr, 43c

ILLUSTRATIONS: Manfred Kostka and Frank Kliemt

Translated by Sue Endsley

COPYRIGHT: © MCMXCVIII Tessloff Publishing, Burgschmietstrasse 2-4, 90419 Nuremberg, Germany
© MCMXCVIII Quadrillion Media LLC, 10105 East Via Linda Road, Suite 103-390, Scottsdale AZ 85258, USA

Visit us on the World Wide Web at http://www.quadrillionusa.com

Library of Congress Cataloging-in-Publication Data is available.

ISBN 1-58185-005-0

Printed in Belgium

Printing 10 9 8 7 6 5 4 3 2 1

Contents

Various species of pilot whales can be found in all oceans. They are still being hunted today in the waters off Japan and the Faeroe Islands.

Ancestry and Body Structure

Even though whales live in the water and look like fish, they are not fish at all, but mammals—marine mammals. They give birth to live young and nurse their young with milk, they breathe air, and they are warm-blooded.

It was in the oceans that life first appeared—approximately three billion years ago. Over time, some plants and animals moved onto land. Some land animals also went back into the water, however, and the ancestors of the whales were among the ones that returned. They were mammals that probably ate insects. When the dinosaurs died out 65 million years ago, they left many environments uninhabited and other types of animals quickly filled these spaces. Around this time the ancestors of the whales started foraging in shallow

Basilosaurus (about 40 million years ago)

Dorudon (about 40 million years ago)

4

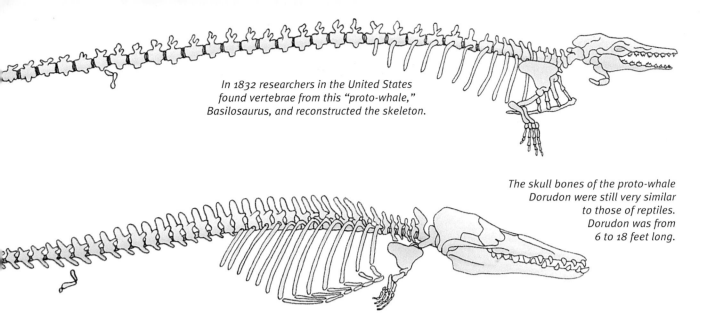

In 1832 researchers in the United States found vertebrae from this "proto-whale," Basilosaurus, and reconstructed the skeleton.

The skull bones of the proto-whale Dorudon were still very similar to those of reptiles. Dorudon was from 6 to 18 feet long.

Approximately 60 million years ago the ancestors of the whales adapted themselves to living in water. Although some of these proto-whales already resembled modern whales, the 66-foot-long Basilosaurus (center) looked more like a serpent.

waters where they probably found a plentiful supply of crustaceans, mollusks, and coastal fish.

The next step in their evolution was the prototype of the modern whale—the "archaeoceti," which spent its whole life in the ocean. Researchers have found fossil remains of these animals in layers of rock that are 50 million years old. They had much shorter hind legs than their land-dwelling ancestors, a long snout, and were about 66 feet long. These were probably the ancestors of the modern toothed and baleen whales. Most species of this prototype whale became extinct 25 million years ago.

Biologists haven't been able to agree on the way they group whales into families. Research during the past decade has shown that some whale species differ in a surprising number of ways from species to which they are supposedly related. Some researchers therefore believe it is quite possible that several different animals returned to the sea and that not all whales have the same ancestors.

Which is the biggest whale?

Some species of whales are real giants. The blue whale, for example, can grow to a length of 108 feet and can weigh as much as 150 tons. It is the largest mammal that ever lived on Earth. Its babies—called "calves"—are about 22 feet long at birth. Fin whales can grow up to 82 feet long. Humpback whales are also enormous—they often reach a length of 47 feet or more. Creatures of this size could probably only evolve in water, since the water supports most of their weight. These giant mammals may have been the sea monsters we find in legends. Centuries ago, when people caught brief glimpses of whales these animals must have seemed terrifying.

One reason whales were able to evolve into such huge animals might be that they have almost no natural enemies. In fact, although baleen whales are among the largest of all, they have no teeth and therefore no means of defense at all. Whales are also very trusting, probably because they never had enemies—until man appeared.

Not all whales are huge, however. The smallest is the black-and-white Commerson's dolphin that lives off the coast of South America. It is usually about 6 feet long.

Right whales are especially slow. That is why they were the first ones to be hunted to the brink of extinction.

The smallest baleen whale is the minke whale, which can grow to 33 feet in length. Whalers began hunting this species in the Antarctic in about 1971 or 1972, since larger species had become rare. Although whaling was banned here in 1994, hunting continues.

The largest animal that ever lived on the Earth is the blue whale. The female of this baleen whale is the larger of the sexes and can be as much as 110 feet long. Because of excessive hunting, blue whales are perilously close to extinction.

A fin whale surfaces for air among ice floes in the Antarctic. Here it finds its chief nourishment: krill.

sperm whale

killer whale

minke whale

blue whale

pilot whale

harbor porpoise

Biologists divide whales (the "order" Cetacea) into two categories or "suborders": toothed whales (Odontoceti) and baleen whales (Mysticeti). Toothed whales have normal teeth and use them to capture and eat fish and squid. Baleen whales have no teeth. Instead, a baleen whale has two horny plates attached to the roof of its mouth. Each of these plates is made up of hundreds of parallel slats with fringed edges. The fringe forms a kind of sieve. As a baleen whale swims, it allows water to flow through these fringed plates, filtering out plankton and small, shrimp-like krill. Gray whales, blue whales, humpback whales, right whales, and fin whales belong to this group.

Toothed whales are predators—they use their teeth for seizing prey. Sperm whales, beaked whales, dolphins, and porpoises belong to this group. Sperm whales are the largest toothed whales and can measure up to 55 feet long. When hunting deep-sea squid, the male of the species can dive 3,000 feet and remain under

What different kinds of whales are there?

There are more than eighty different species of whales, from the small harbor porpoise to the blue whale. Even today biologists still don't know whether toothed whales and baleen whales are distantly related, or if they have simply developed a similar body shape. This streamlined shape, which fish also have, is ideal for life in the water. The tail fin or "flukes" serves as a motor to move the whale through the water.

humpback whale

northern right whale

white-beaked dolphin

white-sided dolphin

fin whale

narwhal

beluga whale

The beluga or white whale lives in the Arctic. Using its back, it can break through the ice that forms over Arctic seas.

water for over an hour. Beluga whales (their name comes from the Russian word for white) and narwhals, on the other hand, live in the shallow waters of the Arctic and feed on swarms of fish or harvest crustaceans, worms, flatfish, and mollusks from the ocean floor. Beluga whales and narwhals have no dorsal fin.

There are several kinds of whales in North American waters. Off the East Coast, you can see humpback whales, fin whales, white-sided dolphins, and, if you are very lucky, one of the few surviving northern right whales. Off the West Coast you can watch the migration of gray whales.

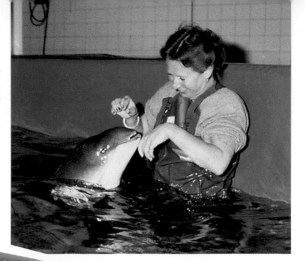

A harbor porpoise that became stranded on the North Sea coast was nursed back to health in the dolphinarium in Harderwijk, Holland.

A fully grown harbor porpoise.

What makes the narwhal different from all other whales is its tusk. Only the males have this tusk, and it can grow up

> **Was the mythical "unicorn" a sea animal?**

to 9 feet long. This is more than half the narwhal's total body length of approximately 16 feet. This ivory tusk has a spiral, twisting shape. In very rare cases, male narwhals may have two tusks. There are even cases of females that have grown a tusk.

In nature, pairs of tusks or horns aren't at all unusual—we find them on wild boars, walruses, and elephants, for example. A formation like the narwhal's single tusk, however, is extremely unusual. Normally narwhals have two teeth in their upper jaw—we don't know

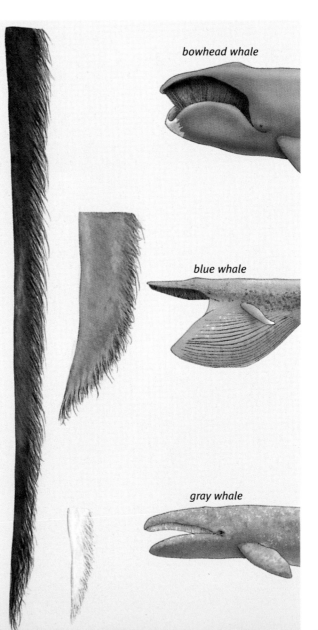

bowhead whale

blue whale

gray whale

The bowhead whale (top) has a deeply curved jaw and long baleen plates (far left). The blue whale (center) has a pleated throat that expands. The gray whale (bottom) has short baleen plates.

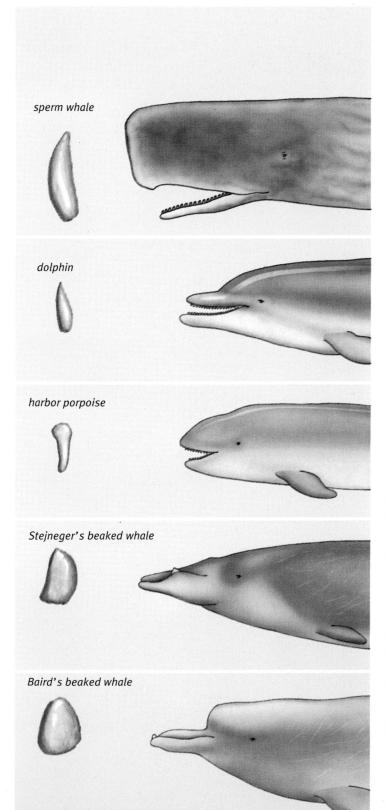

The narwhal, which lives in Arctic waters, is the "unicorn" of the ocean. The tusk of the male has a spiral shape and can reach a length of 9 feet.

sperm whale

dolphin

harbor porpoise

Stejneger's beaked whale

Baird's beaked whale

why only the left one grows into a tusk, and why it only does so in males.

Scientists are still debating whether the narwhal's tusk has any function and, if so, what that function is. Until a few years ago many believed that male narwhals fought each other with their tusks. Recent research suggests it isn't used as a tool or weapon at all, however. Like a deer's antlers or a peacock's feathers, it probably plays a role in choosing a mate.

In the Middle Ages when people found narwhal tusks, they thought these horns came from the legendary unicorn. Many people thought the unicorn's horn possessed medicinal or magical powers. Among other things it was supposed to cure madness, to strengthen the heart, and to be an antidote for any poison. Even today there is widespread belief among some peoples that tusks and horns can work wonders—this is why rhinoceroses are hunted. Collectors and museums also prize narwhal tusks as trophies and showpieces. As a result these animals have been hunted intensely and are now threatened with extinction.

From teeth, scientists can tell more than just the age of a whale; they can also determine its species. Each year the teeth add a layer, forming a growth ring just as trees do. The shape and size of the teeth differ depending on the species.

The bottlenose dolphin was already well known to the Greeks and Romans. Various species of this dolphin can be found in all the world's oceans except for cold polar waters.

Curiosity attracts dolphins to fishing boats, as in this picture taken in the waters off the Azores. By leaping out of the water the dolphins get a better view. In areas where they are still being hunted, however, they have become more cautious.

What are dolphins?

The largest family of toothed whales is that of the dolphins. Thanks to "Flipper," the TV dolphin, they are famous all over the world. Some species live only in tropical waters, but most can be found in oceans around the globe. The pointed snout, the sickle-shaped dorsal fin, and the streamlined body are easy to recognize. They are strong, fast swimmers and are very intelligent. Many species form groups—so-called "schools"—with a high degree of social organization. They seem to have an effective communication system that uses tones of varying pitch.

River dolphins are the only whales that live in fresh water. They can be found in the Ganges, the Indus, the Amazon, the La Plata, and a few Chinese rivers. In these areas the water is so cloudy that good eyesight is of little use. As a result, river dolphins' eyes have become very weak. To compensate for this, however, they have developed a complex echolocation system that they use to get their bearings and to locate prey.

ARTISTS IN ANCIENT GREECE AND ROME often depicted whales and dolphins. It may have been the intelligence of dolphins or their friendliness toward people that made them such popular subjects in paintings and sketches, in sculptures and mosaics. Dolphins also frequently appear on coins, as protectors of travelers.

Bottlenose dolphins lead very social lives. They sometimes carry out acrobatic leaps in unison, just as if they were practicing for a show.

Dolphins leap out of the water to round up shoals of fish— or maybe just for fun.

The Ganges river dolphin lives in fresh water. Since the water it lives in is murky, it uses echolocation to get its bearings. It is almost totally blind.

Why do whales look like fish?

Plants and animals living in the same habitat often develop similar external features, even when they are totally unrelated. This is because they have to adapt to the same set of living conditions. For example, bats and birds aren't at all related—bats are mammals— but both have developed similar structures for flying. Penguins are technically birds, but they have lost the ability to fly and their wings have been transformed into fins—making it possible for them to swim like dolphins. Just as fish did millions of years earlier, whales and seals "discovered" that a streamlined shape is most effective for fast, energy-efficient movement under water. They also "discovered" that in the water flat fins are best suited to steering and propulsion.

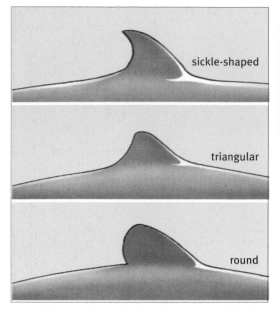

sickle-shaped

triangular

round

Most whales or dolphins have a dorsal fin that serves as a kind of stabilizer while they are swimming. You can usually tell what species a whale belongs to by the shape of its fin.

Why don't whales have legs?

Over millions of years whales became ever better suited to life in the water. The typical skeleton of a mammal—with four legs—changed considerably in the process. Since water supports much of a whale's weight, its skeleton functions less as a support and more as a framework for muscle attachments. Whale bones are porous and comparatively light. They are filled with oil, which reduces the relative density of a whale's body—its density compared to water. Up to half of a whale's body weight may be oil.

The forelegs developed into paddle-shaped pectoral fins or

AS WHALES EVOLVED from land animals, their nostrils gradually moved from the tip of the snout to the top of the head—and became the "blowhole." This makes it possible for whales to swim indefinitely near the ocean's surface and still breathe easily without having to rise higher above the surface. The blowhole of sperm whales is located at the left front of their box-shaped head.

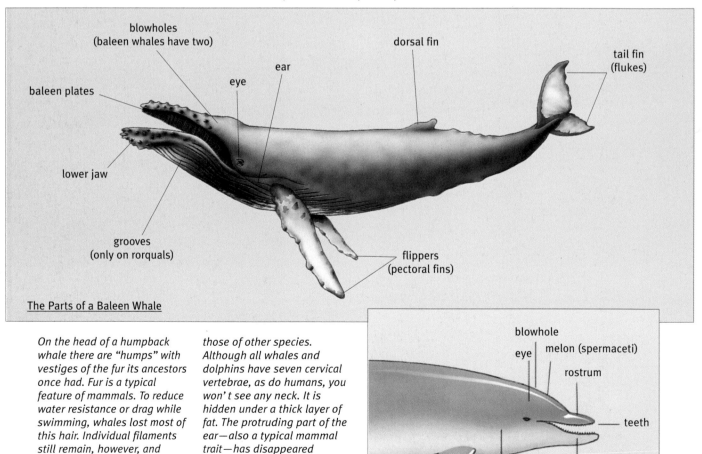

blowholes
(baleen whales have two)

dorsal fin

tail fin
(flukes)

ear

eye

baleen plates

lower jaw

grooves
(only on rorquals)

flippers
(pectoral fins)

The Parts of a Baleen Whale

blowhole

eye

melon (spermaceti)

rostrum

teeth

lower jaw

ear

flipper (pectoral fin)

The Parts of a
Toothed Whale

On the head of a humpback whale there are "humps" with vestiges of the fur its ancestors once had. Fur is a typical feature of mammals. To reduce water resistance or drag while swimming, whales lost most of this hair. Individual filaments still remain, however, and these provide the animal with a sense of touch. The pectoral fins or "flippers" of the humpback whale are longer than those of other species. Although all whales and dolphins have seven cervical vertebrae, as do humans, you won't see any neck. It is hidden under a thick layer of fat. The protruding part of the ear—also a typical mammal trait—has disappeared altogether. Its overall body form is the result of adaptation to life in the water.

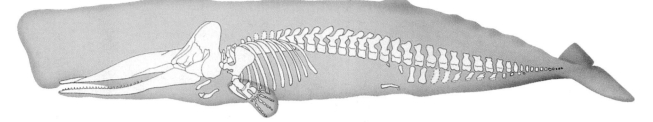

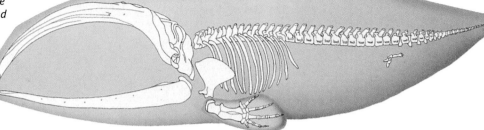

You can clearly see mammal characteristics in the skeletons of the sperm whale (top) and the right whale (bottom)—for example, in the pectoral fins, which still contain all the bones of an arm or front paw.

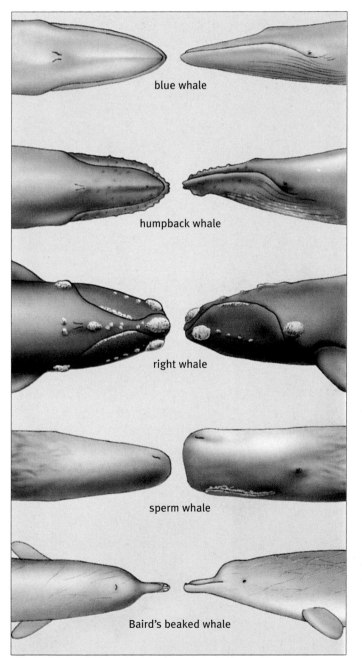

blue whale

humpback whale

right whale

sperm whale

Baird's beaked whale

"flippers." They still have identifiable wrist and finger bones, and they have shortened versions of the bones we have in our arms—the humerus, radius, and ulna. The hind legs, on the other hand, are so atrophied that only a small, walnut-sized bone remains, and even this is often missing. All that's left of the pelvis is a slat-like bone that isn't even connected to the spine any more.

The entire skeleton is designed for a streamlined body. Since its form guarantees minimal water-resistance, the whale can save energy when swimming. In this process of streamlining, the jaws of toothed whales developed into an elongated snout, the seven cervical vertebrae fused together, and the neck disappeared under a thick layer of fat. Body parts that stick out, like ears, also disappeared, and the sexual organs are hidden under folds of skin.

The heads of five typical large whales are shown here from the front (on the left) and from the side. The three at the top are baleen whales, and the two at the bottom are toothed whales. Not only are the shapes of the jaws different, but also the position and shape of the nostrils.

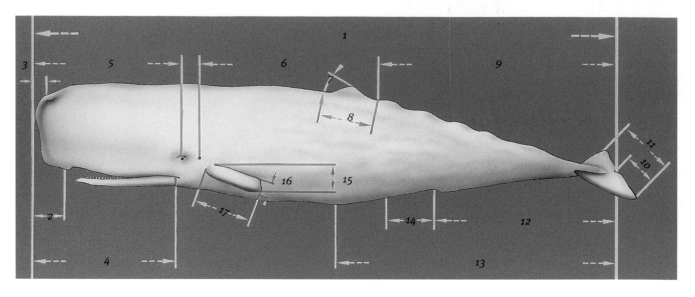

During the transition from life on land to life in the water whales lost their fur. Fur is a typical characteristic of mammals but in the water it didn't have any advantages; in fact, it had several disadvantages. It would have slowed them down, and it would have produced irritating noises as they swam.

Did whales once have fur?

Instead of fur, whales have smooth and very elastic skin. It excretes tiny droplets of a chemical substance that helps the body to glide through the water more easily. This substance also helps prevent the formation of eddies—swirling water currents caused by the motion of the whale through the water. These "counter-currents" slow the whale down. Unlike human skin, the outer layer of whale skin isn't made up of dead skin cells, but of living cells. This helps to reduce water resistance. Since there are also nerve endings in this living skin, it probably serves as a delicate sensory organ as well. With it whales can sense water conditions in the ocean.

To compensate for the loss of their insulating fur, whales have a thick layer of fat, called blubber. In right whales this layer may be as thick as one-and-a-half feet. This fat helps whales maintain the body temperature that other mammals have—between 96.8 and 98.6° F. It also serves as an energy reserve. Without this thick layer of fat whales wouldn't be able to survive

This picture shows how scientists measure whales, here, for example, a sperm whale. They need total body length (1) as well as measurements 2 through 17 in order to classify the animal biologically.

Whales give off excess heat through their skin, especially through their tail fins. This functions in the same way as a car radiator. Cooled blood from vessels near the surface of the flukes circulates back into the interior of the body and can absorb heat there, then return to the surface areas and release the heat.

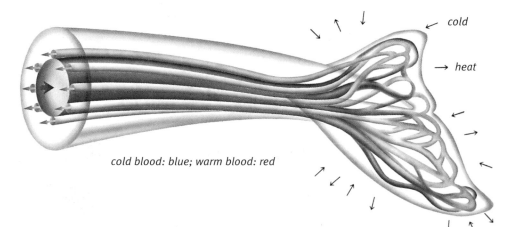

Cold blood circulates into the core of the whale's body and helps regulate body temperature.

← cold

→ heat

cold blood: blue; warm blood: red

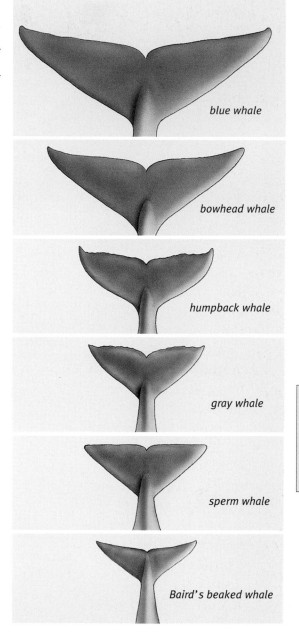

Experts can distinguish different species of whales by the tail fins or "flukes" of diving animals—by the shape and size of the flukes, and sometimes by the color as well. They can even recognize individual animals sometimes by a unique notching or skin coloration.

blue whale

bowhead whale

humpback whale

gray whale

sperm whale

Baird's beaked whale

in the polar regions. The water temperature there is about 32° F.

In warm, tropical waters, however, this "fur coat" of fat would cause a whale's body to overheat, especially when swimming at higher speeds. To prevent this, whales can redirect their blood circulation. If they need to conserve warmth, they limit blood circulation to the inner body, leaving the outer skin cold. If they need to release heat, however, they route part of their blood through an extensive network of blood vessels near the body surface, particularly in the tail fin, and can transfer excess heat into the surrounding water.

How do whales swim?

The part of the body that is most responsible for moving the whale forward is the boneless tail fin, the "flukes." It doesn't stand upright, like the tails of fish, but instead spreads out horizontally and pushes the animal through the water by means of a powerful up and down motion. A bundle of muscles in the whale's tail section supplies the power.

The last thing you see when a whale dives are its flukes—as with the gray whale in this picture. In the background you can see the coast of Baja California, the "nursery" of the gray whales.

17

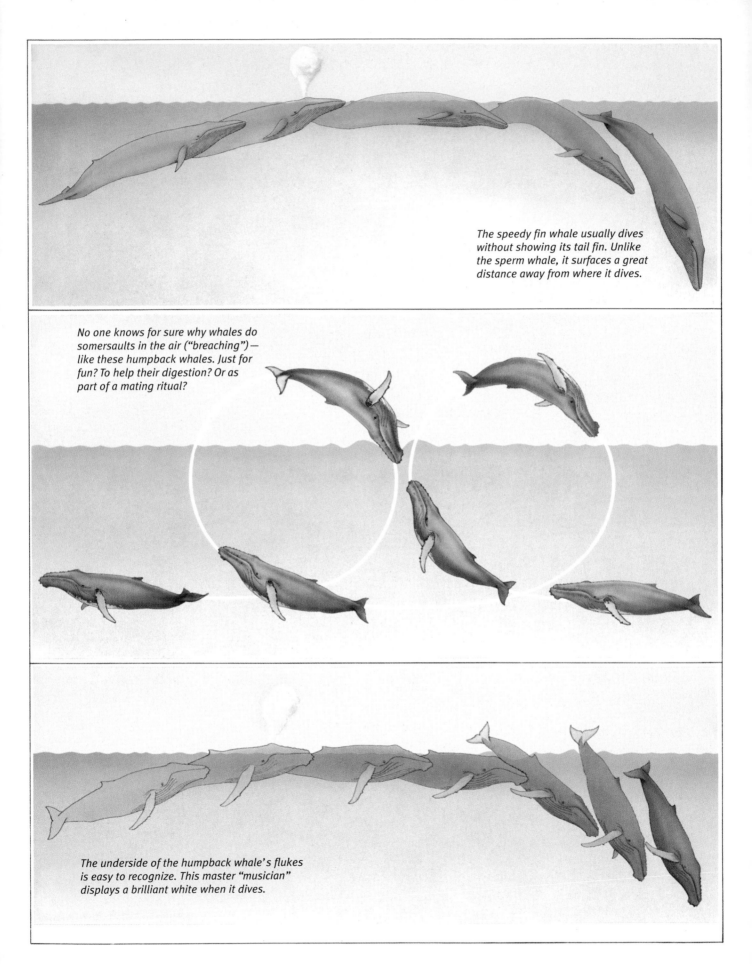

The speedy fin whale usually dives without showing its tail fin. Unlike the sperm whale, it surfaces a great distance away from where it dives.

No one knows for sure why whales do somersaults in the air ("breaching") — like these humpback whales. Just for fun? To help their digestion? Or as part of a mating ritual?

The underside of the humpback whale's flukes is easy to recognize. This master "musician" displays a brilliant white when it dives.

For steering, whales primarily use their pectoral fins (the "flippers"). Using these fins they can control their position in the water. Humpback whales can use their unusually long flippers like propeller blades to rotate their bodies lengthwise.

What do whales eat?

The right whale, one of the baleen whales, makes easy work of feeding. With its mouth wide open it swims through swarms of plankton and krill. Water enters its mouth and flows through the baleen plates. The fringed plates

A fin whale opens its mouth to scoop up plankton-rich water.

Krill is small crustacean about the size of a human thumb and a kind of "bread" for all ocean dwellers in Antarctic waters. They live in huge swarms and humans now fish for them as well.

capture the tiny animals and the water flows out the sides of the mouth. The whale then uses its tongue to collect the animals from the baleen plates.

Whales in the rorqual group use their baleen plates in a different way. They have an expandable throat sack. From their throat to their navel, they have pleated grooves, a bit like an accordion. When a rorqual is hungry it opens its jaws very wide and sucks several tons of plankton-rich water into its elastic throat sack. Then it

snaps its mouth almost shut and presses the water out through the baleen plates, catching the tiny animals in the fringe sieve.

Humpback whales have an especially clever method of hunting. They dive under a swarm of prey and then swim upwards in a spiral, continuously expelling air bubbles. The rising bubbles create a cylinder that "traps" the prey, and the whales can then suck them in through their wide-open mouths.

In the Arctic, a baleen whale's diet consists mainly of krill, sea butterflies, and small fish. In the Antarctic it is almost entirely krill. Here these small, shrimp-like animals form huge swarms. Scientists currently estimate the size of these swarms at about 600 million tons.

One of the baleen whales, the gray whale, prefers shallow, coastal areas and eats mainly animals living on the ocean floor. With its jaws open, it swims along the ocean floor on its side, sucking into its mouth the top inch or two of sand, together with the mussels, worms, and crabs living there. It

Like several of the toothed whales, the sperm whale is a specialist when it comes to food—it mainly feeds on squid. In deep waters large males fight with giant squid that may be up to 55 feet in length— scientists discovered this when they examined the stomach contents of a whale taken by a Russian whaling ship.

SPERM WHALES often swim quietly through the water in small groups, almost like huge zeppelins. Sometimes they float very close to each other on the water's surface. They can float in the water with their head either up or down. These animals have a highly developed echolocation (sonar) system. Researchers suspect that whales at the surface can even detect prey in very deep waters—more than 3,000 feet down. They then build up their supply of oxygen and can dive into the depths with ease.

then pumps the water and sand out through its baleen plates.

While baleen whales graze quite peacefully on plankton, toothed whales are more active hunters. Most of them target shoals of fish, but killer whales also feed on squid, birds, and other marine mammals including smaller whales and seals. Dolphins are especially well known for hunting in groups. They use sounds to round up shoals of fish and then they surround the shoal. Killer whales got their name because of the huge

quantities of animal remains fishermen often found in their stomachs. Although they do attack other whales, they are generally quite peaceful towards humans.

Sperm whales have discovered a special source of food: the giant squid that live in deep waters and are sometimes up to 55 feet long. To get at them, sperm whales must dive at least 3,300 feet—researchers have found drowned sperm whales entangled in deep-sea cables. Some researchers believe these whales can even dive to

YOUNG WHALES ARE EASY PREY for killer whales, so sperm whales sometimes form a defensive ring with their bodies to protect their young. They place their heads together with their tail fins pointing outward—in a so-called "marguerite" (daisy) formation. They put their babies in the center of the ring.

depths of 8,000 feet. Apparently they locate the squid with their echolocation organs. Scars and tentacle marks found on the skin of sperm whales suggest that they often fight bitter battles with their prey in the ocean depths.

To capture the squid they eat, sperm whales not only had to develop special hunting techniques, they also had to adapt their bodies to the demands of deep-sea diving. They have developed systems for storing large quantities of oxygen and a special

How can sperm whales dive so deep and for so long?

organ that makes rapid diving and surfacing possible—the spermaceti organ. This is a huge cushion made of soft, white wax in the sperm whale's head. One of the whale's two nasal passages runs through it—the whale breathes through the other one. This wax has a melting point of 84.2° F. Above this temperature the wax becomes liquid and quite bouyant, but below it, the wax is solid and dense. If the sperm whale wants to dive, it lets the cold surrounding water flow through the nasal passage, bringing the temperature down below 84.2° F. To surface it uses heat from blood vessels in the spermaceti organ to heat the wax back up

Although "Moby Dick," the sperm whale, generally comes to the surface only to breathe and usually spends its time in deep waters looking for food, from time to time it does leap out of the water as dolphins do—for example during mating season.

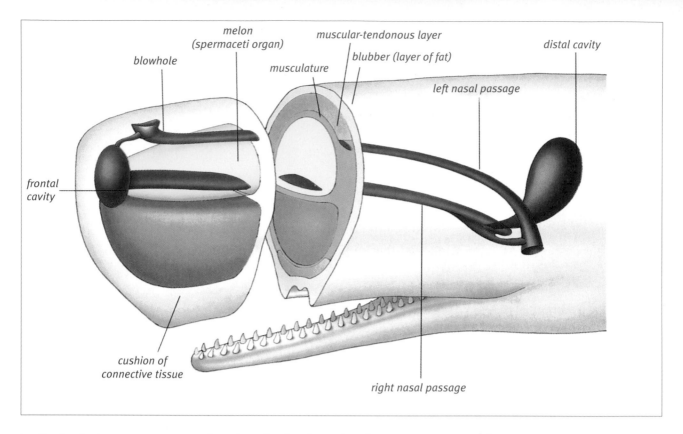

blowhole

melon
(spermaceti organ)

muscular-tendonous layer

distal cavity

musculature

blubber (layer of fat)

left nasal passage

frontal
cavity

cushion of
connective tissue

right nasal passage

to its body temperature, so that it melts and becomes bouyant again.

Before they set out on the hunt, they swim peacefully on the surface for about ten minutes and breathe deeply. The air supplies oxygen to their lungs, and blood from the lungs transports this oxygen to the muscles. They contain a substance similar to the one that gives blood its red color (hemoglobin), called myoglobin, which binds oxygen chemically. During this breathing period, the whale's body fat also becomes saturated with this vital gas.

Once the sperm whale has stored enough oxygen, it tilts headfirst into the chilling water and lets the spermaceti wax become solid. Then it dives.

Sperm whales have only a very small amount of air in their lungs when they dive into deep waters—they exhale almost the entire contents of their lungs before diving. The air sacs in the lungs are covered with a thin layer of cartilage,

This cross-section of a sperm whale head shows the position of the nasal passages and the spermaceti organ—the organ that makes quick diving and resurfacing possible.

The head of a fully-grown sperm whale makes up about one third of its body and contains the "spermaceti organ," a reservoir of wax that is helpful when diving and resurfacing. The eye is extremely small since it is relatively unimportant for diving in deep, dark waters.

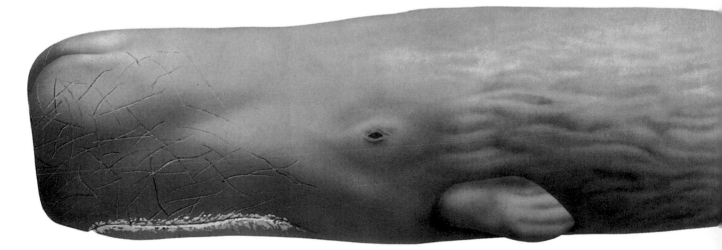

and only a tiny amount of air remains in each sac. This is necessary so the air sacs can expand again as the whale resurfaces. If sperm whales were to take a lot of air down with them, the buoyancy caused by these air bubbles would probably make it impossible to dive quickly. More importantly, however, the whale's body would not be able to withstand the enor-

gen from the air to dissolve in the blood. When the diver rises to the surface, the pressure drops and the nitrogen forms small gas bubbles in the blood. The same thing happens when you open a bottle of soda—the pressure drops and the dissolved gases form bubbles that rise to the surface. These bubbles then block tiny blood vessels. Since whales exhale before diving, there

Fully-grown sperm whale bulls can remain under water for over an hour and at a depth of at least 3,000 feet. They need a good 10 minutes on the surface to "fill up" with oxygen, which they store in their muscles.

mous water pressure. Even at a depth of 330 feet the pressure is about 140 pounds per square inch. Since the sperm whale's oxygen supply doesn't come from air, but rather from oxygen stored in muscles and fat, it also avoids the decompression sickness feared by deep-sea divers—the "bends." Air doesn't just contain oxygen, it is 78% nitrogen, and the high pressure in the ocean depths causes nitro-

is no nitrogen that could do this. When sperm whales dive, their bodily functions slow to a minimum. The myoglobin reservoir supplies oxygen only to the most important organs—brain, spinal cord, and heart. Muscles and other organs must do without oxygen temporarily. A network of blood vessels in the neck and brain seems to be especially important in this respect. It ensures a steady supply of blood to the brain and adjusts blood pressure to match outside water pressure during the dive.

A whale's nostrils aren't at the tip of its snout, but have moved up onto its back in the course of its evolution. This makes it easier for a whale to breathe while swimming. Baleen whales still have two nostrils or blowholes, but on toothed whales these have joined to form a single blowhole.

Why do whales spout?

Normally the blowhole is sealed watertight, but during breathing, muscles open the valve. A second valve at the entrance to the lungs—similar to our larynx—prevents water from coming in through the mouth and throat when whales feed under water.

When they exhale, whales blow air out of their lungs explosively. The sudden expansion cools the air so much that the water vapor in their breath condenses into mist. The shape of this "fountain"—the "spout"—varies from species to species.

How long do whales live?

Only in the cases of a few species do we know how long whales live. This is because scientists have so far only examined whales killed by whalers. With toothed whales it is relatively easy to determine age. Each year a new layer forms on their teeth. In a cross-section of a tooth these layers appear as "year rings" that can be counted. This method doesn't work for baleen whales, however, since they have no teeth—here scientists have to use more complicated procedures.

So far the highest number of rings ever found—70—belonged to a sperm whale. Large bottlenose dolphins like "Flipper" probably live about 40 years.

The food chain in the Antarctic (from bottom to top): zooplankton feeds on phytoplankton; fish, squid, seabirds, and—directly or indirectly—seals and whales feed on zooplankton. Humans harvest from every level of the chain, and usually take too much.

A whale's spout—here of a fin whale—is breath that is released under high pressure and therefore condenses. Experts can recognize a whale by its spout.

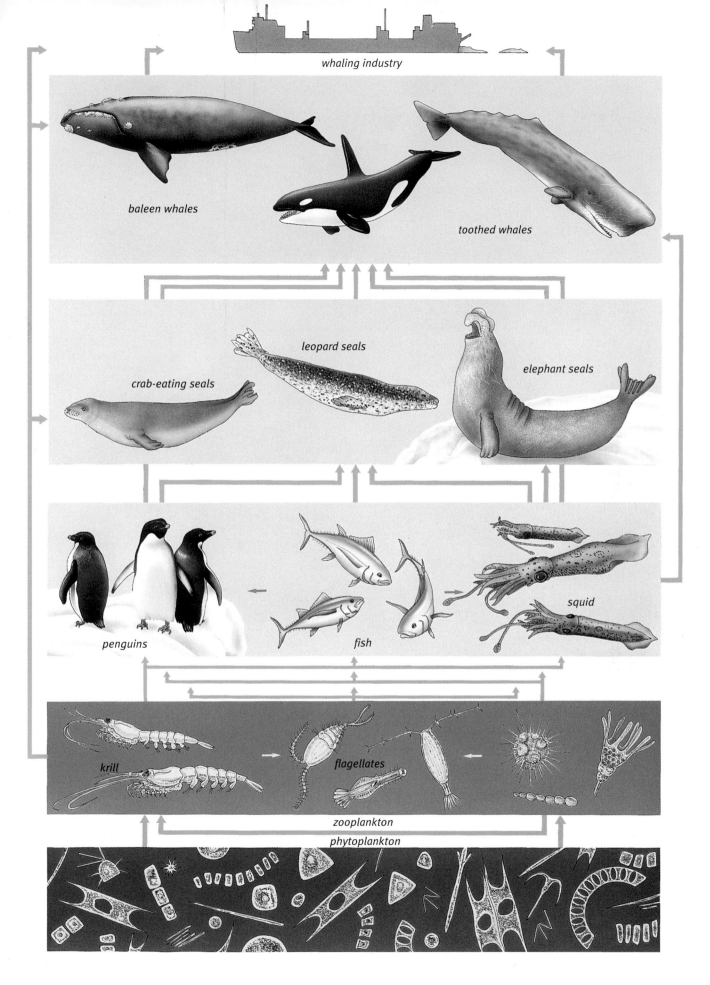

whaling industry

baleen whales

toothed whales

leopard seals

crab-eating seals

elephant seals

penguins

fish

squid

krill

flagellates

zooplankton

phytoplankton

Northern right whales and southern right whales used to be considered the 'right ones' for whalers: they were fat and slow and therefore easy to catch. They need their thick layer of blubber to keep warm.

What role do whales play in the ocean economy?

By the time they are fully-grown, large baleen whales have few natural enemies in their own habitat. This is why they are such peaceful creatures. They feed relatively low down in the food chain, consuming plankton, the tiny life forms of the seas.

According to rough estimates, before whalers appeared on the scene, baleen whales consumed over 300 million tons of Antarctic krill a year—approximately half of the entire krill population. Krill is also the staff of life for seals, penguins, squid, and deep-sea creatures.

The toothed sperm whales play a similar role as the single most important enemy of deep-sea squid—there really aren't any other animals capable of hunting at such depths. Basically, the fish consumption of toothed whales is insignificant considering the size of the oceans and rich sources of

Gray whale babies do not mind being petted when they are a little bigger.

food they contain. Overfishing has always been a human specialty—it occurs only in areas where humans use modern fishing methods to exploit the oceans.

Whales don't just consume, however, they provide living space for others: they are themselves moving habitats. This is especially true of slow-swimming coastal species—gray whales, for example. The broad surface of their skin supports a colorful variety of ma-

Sense Organs

rine life. In addition to small diatoms, huge numbers of barnacles and goose barnacles establish themselves on the whale's skin. They filter their food from the water and their traveling host constantly transports them to new feeding grounds.

Eel-like lampreys attach themselves to whales with their suckers, and "whale lice," tiny crustaceans less than an inch long, creep around between the barnacles. These are true parasites and feed on blood, skin, and probably waste products as well. As a result, they especially like to settle around wounds and body openings.

Sea birds value the whale as a feeding ground because of these parasites and like to perch on swimming whales.

Although mammals typically have good eyesight, this wasn't much help to whales after they moved from land back to water. Water is too dense, and often too cloudy, for good visibility, and light doesn't penetrate very deep beneath the ocean's surface. Of course, above water eyes are very useful. Killer whales often "stand" up out of the water for a look around—perhaps to watch an approaching ship or to look for food—an unsuspecting seal on an ice floe, for example.

The sense of smell isn't of much use under water either, since it reacts only to gas-like substances—molecules not bound into a liquid

How do whales find their food?

Whales can also be "marketed" live—for example, on whale watches organized for tourists.

Gray whales were considered virtually extinct, before they were finally protected along the coasts of the United States and Mexico. This protection came too late for stocks off Asia and in the Atlantic, however.

dolphin

squid

killer whale

or solid. So a whale uses its nose only for breathing, and the mucous membranes and the area of the brain associated with smell have atrophied. Whales can taste things, however. They use their sense of taste to determine the salt content of the water around them or to identify other members of their species by their urine—whales urinate often to remove excessive salt from their bodies.

To compensate for the senses that have become weak, toothed

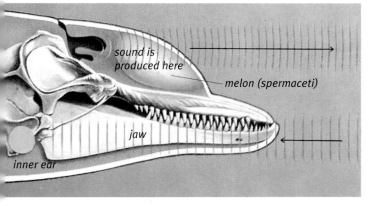

sound is produced here

melon (spermaceti)

jaw

inner ear

The "melon" is an important organ for echolocation. It is a cushion of fat in the fore-head cavity and seems to focus outgoing sound waves. Incoming echoes are apparently conveyed to the ear through the lower jaw.

whales have developed a very effective echolocation system—something we have only known about for a few years now. With this system they can even detect small prey and swim straight for them—much as another mammal, the bat, does in the air. They also use this "sonar" to orient themselves in the water.

This system uses sound signals with frequencies as high as 280 kilohertz. Such "ultrasound" is well outside the range of our hearing—it only reaches as high as 18 kilohertz. Nevertheless, with the help of underwater microphones and special equipment, sound engineers have made it possible for human beings to "hear" these signals. When made audible to us, they sound like rapid clicking—anywhere from five to five hundred clicks per second.

The sound seems to come from the nasal passages. There are several narrow spots in these pas-

It probably takes a whale about two seconds to assess its surroundings and locate prey with its sonar system. Whales "see" to a certain extent with their ears. This acoustic orientation system functions across distances as great as 5,000 feet.

NOISE POLLUTION is also a problem for whales. As ships, underwater mining, and offshore drilling become more numerous, the seas are becoming noisier and noisier, even in deep waters. Researchers fear that whales, which have very sensitive hearing organs, will suffer more and more from such noise. Loud noises not only interfere with their sense of hearing temporarily, they can also cause permanent damage.

sages, and if a whale blows a sharp burst of air through these narrowings, the air vibrates. A whale can probably push a small amount of air back and forth through these narrow spots to make sounds and still save air during long dives.

In the forehead and snout of toothed whales there is a large round mass of fat and waxes called the "melon." For a long time its function was a mystery to scientists. Now they assume that this organ acts as an acoustic lens, concentrating the ultrasound waves and projecting them forward. Animals, cliffs, the ocean surface, and the ocean floor all change and reflect these "acoustic radar signals" in different ways. Whales receive the returning echoes with ears located behind their eyes, and their brain processes them to form an image of the surroundings.

This echolocation system is very precise. As we know from dolphins held in captivity, they can locate fine wires in the water—wires only a few hundredths of an inch thick. They can also distinguish between two balls of only slightly different size—a difference so slight that humans can't see it with the naked eye. They can probably recognize friends or foes from a long way off, track down shoals of fish, and assess the size, type, and even health of another animal. Returning sound waves pass into the interior of their body and may provide dolphins with a kind of "X-ray" image.

It is unfortunate, however, that many whales—and also seabirds, turtles, and seals—are unable to recognize the synthetic nets used by the modern fishing industry. As a result, millions of animals each year die in agony—drowning in these nets.

Using air bubbles they expel from their noses, humpback whales "invented" fishing with nets. Krill and plankton are apparently fooled into thinking they are trapped in the exhaled net of bubbles—and are easy prey for whales.

What is the purpose of whales' songs?

All species of whales use sounds to communicate with each other. For such communication they generally use frequencies that lie within the range of human music. We call them "whale songs" but they also include clicking, grunting, snoring, groaning, and chirping sounds. Since they are created under water they can't really be heard out of the water. In earlier times, the hulls of wooden ships picked up these vibrations and conveyed them to the sailors within. They couldn't explain where the sounds came from, however, and many of them believed they were listening to "mermaids" singing.

Humpback whales are especially good singers. Their songs sound melodic even to human ears—you can actually buy recordings of them. The melodies consist of ordered series of themes and movements and can go on for more than thirty minutes. If a whale interrupts its song, for whatever reason, it picks it up again at exactly the same place. Each animal's song shows unique characteristics, but during a certain season of the year all whales in the same area sing the same song. In other regions whales sing in clearly distinct "dialects." Over time these melodies change and whales leave out some themes and add new verses. Since water is a good conductor of sound, whale songs can be heard over enormous distances. The songs are often audible within an 18-mile radius. The clicking and groaning noises are even audible as far as 125 miles away.

Since whales sing most frequently during the mating season, and in the areas where they reproduce, it is quite likely that their songs play a role in finding a partner. It is also possible that baby whales recognize and find their mothers by their songs.

Why do whales become stranded?

Every few years we see an article in a newspaper describing a mass stranding, often involving several dozen whales. Especially on the East Coast of North America and along the coasts of Australia and New Zealand there are stretches where schools of whales again and again

TIME AND AGAIN, not just a single whale, but a whole group of whales becomes stranded. For a long time scientists have been trying to explain why this happens. Many now believe that these are "road accidents." Some whales, such as pilot whales, seem to orient themselves according to the lines of force in the Earth's magnetic field. The strength of this magnetic field varies slightly, and the patterns of these variations create a kind of map that allows whales to find their way in the water. Near the coast, however, there are often disturbances of these magnetic fields. These disturbances confuse animals that are used to the high seas, causing them to swim into shallow waters. These

The humpback whale has extremely long flippers which serve as underwater propellers when it rolls in the water lengthwise.

magnetic disturbances might also explain why the whales sometimes swim back to these deadly shallows even after animal protection groups have returned them to the open seas. Since they won't abandon any member of the herd, they swim together to their deaths.

end up in water that is too shallow. In 1970, for example, 59 sperm whales were washed up on Okita Beach in New Zealand within a two-hour period. In January of the same year 150 false killer whales were stranded on the coast of Florida.

Such catastrophes usually occur in areas with flat, underwater sandbanks, and they often involve pilot whales. This is presumably because pilot whales live in particularly close-knit social groupings.

If a single animal panics near a flat coast and races towards land, the others follow blindly. The flat, muddy banks also send back a very indistinct echo, and the whales' echolocation system doesn't warn them soon enough.

Once they are stranded on the sand and mud, it is too late. The water no longer supports them, and their bodies collapse under their own weight. The whales can no longer inflate their lungs and they therefore soon suffocate.

Some whales can't detect their echoes in shallow, muddy water and become stranded. Without help they suffocate and die under the weight of their own bodies. Even when people try to help, it usually doesn't do any good.

Migratory Routes and Reproduction

Marine life isn't spread evenly throughout the oceans. Tropical waters are warm but don't contain many nutrients and so there is little plankton and few fish. The polar oceans, on the other hand, are rich in nutrients, since mineral-rich water is constantly rising from the ocean floor. The water there is also well supplied with oxygen since gases dissolve more easily in cold water than in warm. Finally, polar waters provide a good environment for micro-algae since the sun shines constantly, at least in the summer months.

The effect of these factors is especially strong in Antarctic waters. As a result, there are huge swarms of krill there. These tiny animals feed on plankton—in particular on green diatoms—and are the staff of life for many, many animals. It's no wonder both baleen and toothed whales like to romp in the polar oceans in the summer despite the extremely cold water. Besides—they are protected from the cold by their thick layer of blubber.

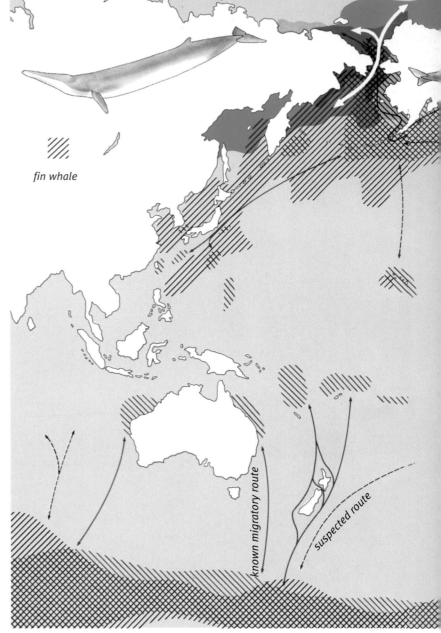

fin whale

known migratory route

suspected route

Most whales spend summer in the food-rich polar regions (both north and south) and return to warmer areas for the mating season.

The calves of many large whales don't yet have the thick, insulating blubber their parents do and would die in icy waters. Whales therefore mate and nurse their young in warmer waters. They go to polar waters only to feed and build up their cushion of blubber.

Gray whales have an especially strong migratory drive. Several thousand of them still live off the West Coast of North America. The Korean and Atlantic gray whales have both been exterminated. In the western Pacific, they were still being killed as late as 1966.

Female gray whales conceive their young between December and February in shallow lagoons

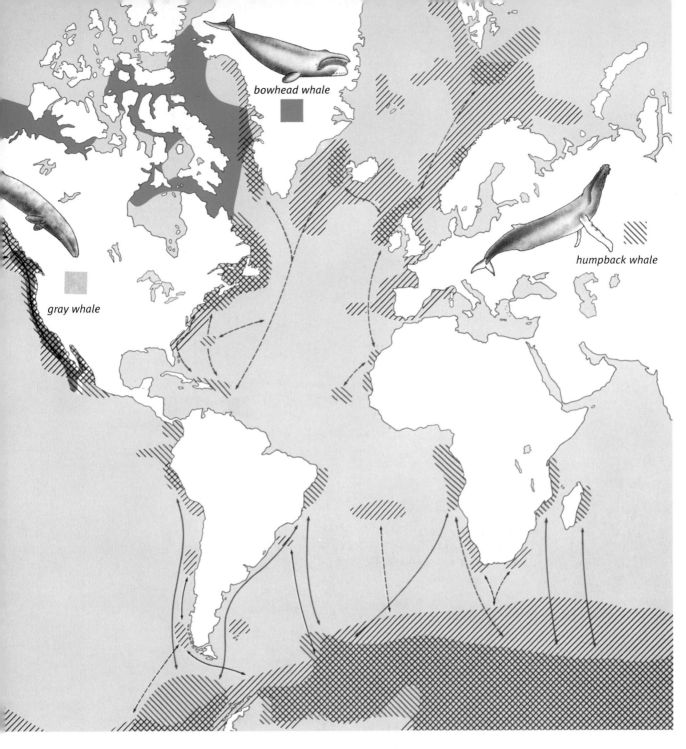

bowhead whale

humpback whale

gray whale

THE LONG-DISTANCE RECORD among mammals is held by gray whales—each year they migrate more than 6,000 miles. They swim an average of 5 miles per hours, but can reach speeds up to 12.5 miles per hour over short distances.

along the coast of Baja California. Between March and May they migrate northwards to the Bering Sea. There they feed, putting on as much fat as possible by October—about half their weight. In November they return to Baja California—after a 13-month pregnancy—and give birth to a single baby. In March they go North again. In warm, nutrient-poor waters they

use up much of their fat reserve and now have to replenish it.

These whales swim at about five miles per hour. In an emergency, however, they can swim at speeds up to 12 miles per hour, but only for short periods. A migration from California to the Arctic and back covers approximately 6,000 miles, giving gray whales the long-distance record among mammals.

How are baby whales born?

Some of the large whale species are sexually mature at six years of age. The females then bear a single calf every two years—twins are very rare. Mating takes place after an extended courtship. The animals stroke each other with their bodies and flippers and bite each other playfully on the snout or on the tail fins. After a pregnancy period of between 10 and 16 months—depending on the species—a calf is born.

No one has ever witnessed the birth of a large whale. What little we know about this underwater event has come from females living in captivity. Apparently the

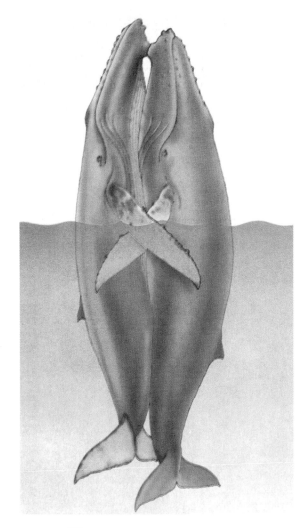

umbilical cord

afterbirth

Unlike most other mammals, whales are born in the "breach" position, coming into the world flukes first. In the case of a long labor it seems that survival chances—for a marine animal that breathes with lungs—are higher if the baby is born in this way.

other females in the herd form a protective circle around the mother-to-be when labor pains start. Whale young are born with their tail fins first—in contrast to nearly

Like these humpback whales, whales generally have sensitive skin and enjoy body contact. This is especially true during the mating season when males and females join together and "stand up." With their flippers around each other it looks as if they are "hugging."

Gray whale babies often like to climb up on mother's broad back for a little break when they are tired from their first "swimming lessons." In Baja California tourists can watch this show.

WHALES THAT LIVE IN GROUPS, as dolphins do, have developed behavioral patterns that strengthen the ties within the group. These animals swim side by side, leap or "breach" in unison, and rise to the surface together in order to breathe. By turning their heads and bodies they greet each other and say good-bye. Touch is also very important. Whales rub sides or stomachs together, and bump each other with their snouts. At times they also have fights.

all large land mammals and also human beings, where the head normally comes first. The umbilical cord is not bitten off, but tears by itself when the baby swims free of its mother. The mother pushes it gently up to the surface where it takes its first breath.

As soon as the calf is born it is, for the most part, independent. It still receives milk from its mother and a certain amount of protection from enemies, but it has to swim on its own from the very start. Of course, a newborn blue whale calf, at a length of 23 feet, and a weight of about 4,400 pounds, doesn't have many enemies to fear.

On the average, mother whales nurse their calves from four (small dolphins) to 13 months (sperm whales). The teats are concealed in folds of skin and the pressure of the milk pushes them out. A baby dives down under its mother's stomach to nurse, takes one of the teats in its mouth, and

How long do baby whales stay with their mothers?

presses with its tongue against its gums until milk flows. Whale milk is extremely high in fat, protein, and minerals. As a result, whale calves grow very quickly. In seven months a blue whale calf grows about 30 feet in length, and each day it adds about 220 pounds! It also builds up the protective layer of blubber it will need when it swims into polar seas—while still only a few months old.

At first calves stay very close to their mothers, who swim quite slowly. Only after a few weeks do they swim away on short excursions. Over time they learn to roll, to lie on their backs, and to jump out of the water.

Before whales set off on their migration, the mothers practice speed swimming with their young. We don't know if calves feed on their own during the summer in the polar regions. We are certain that they continue nursing while their mothers replenish their layer of blubber and prepare for their next pregnancy. After they return to the warm Californian waters the whale mothers wean their calves.

Whales are seldom loners. They usually form herds—"schools" or "pods"—sometimes including dozens of animals. By doing this they can better protect their young. Killer whales, for example, live in families composed of males and females of various generations. Even most baleen whales migrate in groups through the polar seas, although they separate to feed on krill and plankton. Smaller toothed whales organize group hunts for shoals of fish. Apparently they catch more using this method than when hunting alone. They swim close to each other, driving the fish together by whistling, beating their flukes on the water, and making eating noises, and then snap up the fattest members of the shoal of fish. On occasion, they even drive a catch of fish into a fisherman's nets in this way.

Female sperm whales and their young form social groups that stay in temperate latitudes. While most of the females are off hunting under water, one or two remain behind with the young, who cannot yet dive this deep. As soon as young males are sexually mature, around the age of ten, they leave the herd of females and join a group of other young males. Although they are now capable of reproducing, they have to wait until they are about 25 years old, at which point they are also "socially mature." Only then do they mate with the females. The reason for this separation of the sexes might be that the males, who are twice as heavy as females, don't want to make the females compete for food.

Why do whales live in groups?

When dolphins sense danger, they stay underwater close to each other like a school of fish. This provides them better protection.

Behavior

Are dolphins friends of man?

"A man named Koiranos," an old Greek story tells us, "met several fishermen who were getting ready to kill a dolphin that had become entangled in their net. Koiranos persuaded them to stop and, after giving the fishermen some money, set the dolphin free. A short time later the ship he was on was wrecked near the island of Mykonos. Koiranos was the only person to survive the accident—he was saved by a dolphin and carried to the beach."

There are also Roman and Polynesian stories about dolphins helping people in danger. Even in recent times there have been plenty

For many ancient people the dolphin was considered to be a symbol of the sea's vital energy. This Greek bowl shows Dionysus together with dolphins.

Like dolphins, sperm whales help each other when they are ill—or, as in this picture, when they are attacked by humans. Following the motto "together we stand" these very socially minded animals close ranks when they are in danger or threatened, and even stick together to the death.

for the whales, since whalers finding them in this formation can easily shoot them one by one. Despite centuries of slaughter, whales are still friendly towards humans, even though they have learned from bad experiences and no longer swim up to ships as trustingly as they once did. The author of this book has personally experienced sperm whales off the coast of Madeira and the Azores coming up alongside her boat to play and then allowing her to stroke them. Off the coast of California there are whale watches on which tourists can watch gray whales on their migrations.

Since ancient times there have been stories that dolphins have helped fishermen with their work. The Soviet whale researcher, Avenir Tomilin, reported an encounter between a dolphin and a Russian fishing trawler. The dolphin was caught in their nets by mistake and was released. Many days later it returned to the ship and started jumping out of the water, presumably to catch their attention. The fishermen realized the reason when they turned on their sonar: it showed a huge shoal of fish.

of reports about such incidents. In 1943 the American magazine "Natural History" described an incident off the Florida coast: a woman had become unconscious while swimming and could only recall someone bumping her quite forcefully and then pushing her to the beach.

Dolphins also do the same thing for members of their own species who are ill or have had an accident. They hold them at the surface of the water so that they can breathe. Sperm whales circle round a harpooned or injured member of their species, forming a so-called marguerite formation. This behavior has unfortunate consequences

Scientists have been struggling for years now to try and assess the intelligence of dolphins. Their brain is about the same size and of about the same complexity as a human brain, and it is very likely that dolphins are almost as intelligent as we are. However, we still have no way of measuring this.

It is certain that they are not led purely by instinct, and they clearly have a sophisticated, acoustic communication system. It is so complicated that, so far, all our attempts to decipher it have failed—even using super computers. The range of

Whales and dolphins are a sensation in shows all over the world. Certainly such animals help raise awareness and understanding among humans, but these "sprinters of the sea" are rarely happy in captivity.

Keiko, the whale from the movie Free Willy, has thrilled many children. Like Keiko, killer whales often suffer from lack of movement in captivity and their back fins become limp.

frequencies used in their communication is ten times that of human speech. We don't even know the extent of their vocabulary. From observations in dolphinariums, however, we do know that they can

transmit astonishingly complicated orders and descriptions without eye contact. For example, a dolphin can react to a visual signal even when blindfolded because its partner "whispers" the command to it.

They don't seem to experience the problem of "foreign" languages—the dolphin language is the same worldwide. If researchers play them recordings of their language, they stop answering after a short time. Apparently the language no longer fits the context—they can't be tricked that easily.

At other times, however, they show little rationality. For example, they allow themselves to be surrounded and caught in nets, even when it would be easy for them to jump over the edge of the net and escape to freedom.

For more than 100 years now humans have been capturing live whales and putting them on display. In 1874 visitors to

Can dolphins be trained?

For more than 100 years now humans have been capturing live whales and putting them on display. In 1874 visitors to Boston could see a beluga whale kept in a large tank. The whale performed tricks and let visitors pet it. In 1912 an aquarium in New York exhibited dolphins, and in 1938 the first oceanarium opened in St. Augustine, Florida. The dolphins attracted huge crowds. Word got around and today there are dolphinariums around the world. Besides dolphins, some also keep killer whales, pilot whales, and even baleen whales.

These animals perform a wide variety of tricks. They throw balls into baskets, jump through hoops high over the water, do headstands or "walk" on their tail fins, and let their trainers ride on their backs.

Trainers usually begin by watching a dolphin for some desired behavior—like a jump. After the dolphin displays the behavior—by chance, of course—the trainer blows a whistle and "rewards" the animal with a piece of fish. Soon the dolphin connects "whistle" with "reward." Now the trainer can move to more complicated tricks. To get it to jump through a hoop, for example, a trainer hangs a hoop in the water and rewards the animal when it happens to swim through the hoop. The trainer then raises the hoop.

Dolphin Reef at Elat, Israel, is a 12,000-square-yard enclosure for dolphins in a natural environment. Through a permanently open 'door' dolphins can swim in and out of the Red Sea as they please.

After every performance in the dolphinarium the acrobats wait for a fish as a reward. To keep them motivated, they are often given very little.

If dolphins have to live in captivity, then regular and playful contact between animal and trainer is certainly important.

Captive dolphins get sick easily and dolphinariums regularly need replacement animals. To capture a dolphin, a team surrounds it, catches it in a net, and carefully pulls it onto the beach. It is lifted onto soft mats, loaded into a helicopter or plane, and transported to its new home. New animals are kept in special tanks for observation. Some can't adjust to captivity and are freed.

There are many animals, that die at the time of capture or while being transported to the tank—from shock or stress or occasionally from overheating. In transit they usually don't have the water they need to cool their bodies, and they can't sweat to cool themselves.

Hunting Whales and Protecting Whales

Who was Moby Dick?

Every once in a while, a whale is born without any skin pigments—an "albino" whale. One such whale was the main character of a novel written by Herman Melville in 1851: "Moby Dick"—a white sperm whale. The captain of a whaling ship, Captain Ahab, tries again and again to kill this extraordinary white giant, but it always escapes. The obsessed Ahab does not give up, however, and pursues the whale around the world. Finally he manages to harpoon the whale, but the whale cannot be stopped and pulls him down into the deep. Melville himself took part in some whaling expeditions, and his tales are not simply exciting, they are also very true to life.

How long have humans been hunting whales?

Ever since there have been whales, there have been whales that became stranded. Thousands of years ago, people living along the coasts probably saw the enormous amounts of fat and meat that suddenly appeared before them as a gift from the sea god. They ate the meat, used the whale oil as fuel, and the bones as building materials. Later unusually brave souls ventured out to hunt whales swimming near the coast. The Vikings may have been the first whalers. We know for sure that the Basques had made a business of harpooning right whales in the Bay of Biscay as early as the 12th century. The barbed spear used by whalers—

HUNTING AND EXTINCTION—

About 40 years of intensive whale fishing in the Atlantic—using modern equipment—were enough to drive the large blue whale almost to extinction. That's why this animal was declared an endangered species and put under protection in 1966. In spite of this, only a few hundred blue whales survive in the Southern hemisphere today. We also know that whalers have continued to hunt this animal.

It has barely been 400 years since the beginning of commercial whaling in the Arctic—as seen in many historical engravings. In the course of two centuries whalers using hand harpoons killed off the slow right whales.

the "harpoon"—gets its name from the Basque word "arpoi," which means "catch fast." Since the body of the dead whale floated, thanks to its thick layer of blubber, it was easy for whalers to tow it to the beach, where they then cut it up.

Soon "coastal" whales became scarce and the Basques extended their whaling areas further and further. They improved their tools, built better ships, and by 1372 had reached as far as Newfoundland. They actually reached the American continent long before Columbus.

Other nations such as England, France, Spain, and Holland soon took part in the large-scale round-up of these giants of the sea and pursued them even into the Arctic.

Every spring fleets of whalers left their harbors. The whalers drove herds of right whales, bowheads and northern right whales into narrow channels of water between islands and then harpooned them until the water ran red with blood. On the coasts they set up temporary whaling stations where they cut the blubber into pieces and then heated it until it "rendered" into whale oil. This was then filled into barrels and loaded onto the ship. In the Dutch whaling town of Smeerenburg on Amsterdam Island near Spitsbergen, 300 men were kept busy in good years. There were also bars and gambling halls for the whalers.

Whaling was good business, and many ship owners became

Up until 1981 whalers from Madeira hunted sperm whales in homemade sloops.

The helmsman and the harpooner—here from the neighboring Azores—are the most important men in the boat.

As soon as a whale surfaces the harpooner keeps its back in his sights.

rich. It was also very dangerous, however, and not just for whales. Ships might sink in storms, or be crushed by icebergs, or be trapped among ice floes when winter arrived unexpectedly and the sea froze. Many whalers died in the polar seas.

Despite the comparatively primitive hunting methods used, the whale population began to disappear off the Arctic coast after only a few decades. Whalers followed the right whales out to open sea and towed them back to land or to an ice floe to cut them up. At the beginning of the eighteenth century, when bowhead whales and northern right whales had become rare, American, British and Dutch whalers started hunting sperm whales in the warmer oceans of the world. The heyday of sperm whale hunting was between 1820 and 1850. After this, the sperm whale population was severely depleted. More importantly, however, a cheaper alternative to whale oil and whale candles appeared—petroleum. This put an end to most of the whaling industry for the moment.

A converted fishing cutter serves as a kind of factory ship and during the night takes the dead whales to the station on land for processing the next day.

How were these "giants of the sea" killed?

The whaling industry didn't remain quiet for long, however. The Norwegians soon turned their interest to the rorquals, which were too fast to be caught with traditional hand harpoons. Thanks to steam ships and the harpoon gun, developed by the Norwegian Svend Foyn in 1864, they too soon became easy prey. Highly accurate grenade harpoons

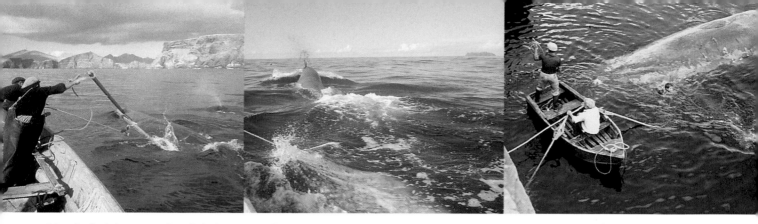

When he is right next to the whale he throws the hand harpoon, which lodges in the blubber, then he grabs the lance...

He lunges with the lance again and again until the whale spouts blood and breathes its last breath...

The carcass is towed to the landing station and pulled on land the next day for processing.

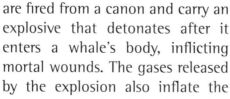

The harpoon gun with explosive head was invented in the late 19th century. It explodes inside the whale and inflates its body, so that species like the fast-swimming rorquals (blue whales, minke whales, and fin whales) don't sink to the ocean floor after they die. The "native population" of Greenland is partly freed from the ban on whaling. Since it is part of their traditional culture they are allowed to take a certain number of whales each year—even though they, too, have modern harpoons and boats.

First the sperm whale's blubber is cut off and then the meat is processed. Masses of blood pour out onto the platform.

are fired from a canon and carry an explosive that detonates after it enters a whale's body, inflicting mortal wounds. The gases released by the explosion also inflate the whale's body so that it doesn't sink. If you could still use the word "hunt" to describe earlier whaling techniques, then this new invention transformed whaling into mass slaughter.

As whaling ships began penetrating the Antarctic, the whales' last refuge disap-

peared. By 1910 there were already six whaling stations on the islands off the Antarctic coast, and a further 14 factory ships working in the same area. In one year alone, 48 whaling ships took 10,230 whales. In 1925 the first "factory whaling ship" started work. Whalers pulled the dead whales up the stern ramp onto the deck of this "floating whaling station," and then carried out the entire process of cutting and processing the whales right on the ship.

Today there are no more hiding places for whales. The times are long gone when a look-out located whales from the crow's nest,

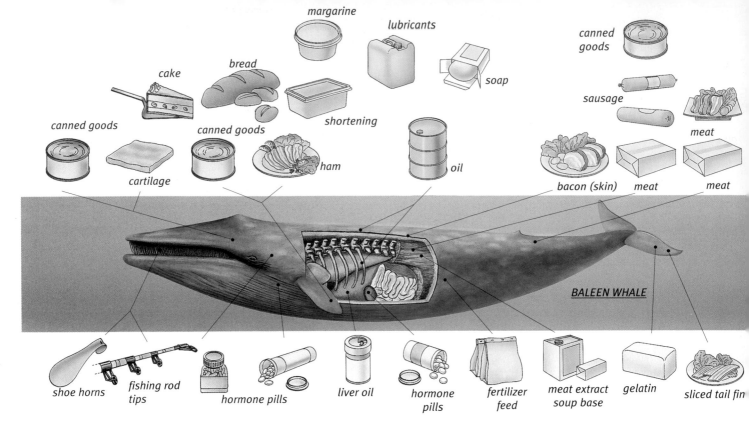

margarine

lubricants

canned goods

cake

bread

soap

canned goods

shortening

sausage

canned goods

meat

cartilage

ham

oil

bacon (skin)   meat   meat

BALEEN WHALE

shoe horns

fishing rod tips

hormone pills

liver oil

hormone pills

fertilizer feed

meat extract soup base

gelatin

sliced tail fin

high up on the mast, and announced them by shouting: "Whale! There she blows!" With today's observation helicopters and advanced radar and echolocation systems the whales no longer have a chance.

What products do we get from whales?

Modern processing methods exploit virtually every part of the whale. The days are long gone when whale oil was used to fuel lamps and when "whalebone" (the baleen) was used for making umbrellas, corset stays, hatboxes, and other items. Whale meat is considered a delicacy in Japan and is used in some other countries as animal feed. Spermaceti or sperm oil is a much sought-after lubricant for industrial use, since it can withstand the high temperatures in high-performance engines. It is also used as base for cosmetics. The

bones are boiled down for glue or ground up for fertilizers, or they are processed into "fish meal"—as is the inedible meat of the sperm whale. Tourist shops sometimes sell "scrimshaw"—sperm whale teeth decorated with intricate carvings—as souvenirs. Ambergris—a nearly odorless, dark mass found in the intestines of sperm whales—is highly valued as a base for producing perfumes.

Japan, in particular, still uses many products derived from baleen whales (left) and sperm whales (right). There are good substitutes for all of these products. In addition to its own production, Japan also imports more of these same products from other whaling nations.

Ambergris is sometimes found in the intestines of sperm whales. It once served as a base for perfumes.

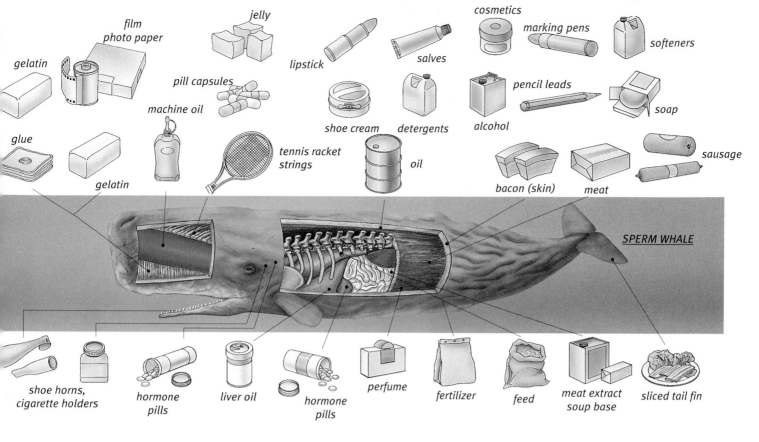

gelatin

film photo paper

jelly

lipstick

cosmetics

marking pens

salves

softeners

glue

pill capsules

machine oil

gelatin

tennis racket strings

shoe cream

detergents

alcohol

pencil leads

soap

oil

bacon (skin)

meat

sausage

SPERM WHALE

shoe horns, cigarette holders

hormone pills

liver oil

hormone pills

perfume

fertilizer

feed

meat extract soup base

sliced tail fin

Spermaceti is found in the frontal caves of sperm whales. It is melted—"rendered"—to make sperm oil, and is very valuable to the cosmetic and lubricant industries.

The nut of the jojoba, a plant native to semi-desert areas, contains a substance that can be substituted for sperm oil.

Do we really need whale products?

Because of the variety and quantity of products they supply, whales have always been valuable prey. Today, however, there are alternatives to every whale product. Whale meat isn't a basic foodstuff, not even in Japan, the primary market for such meat. It is a rare delicacy and represents about 0.01 percent of all protein consumed in Japan. In cosmetics, sperm oil was replaced long ago by vegetable fats and oils. We now use primarily synthetic substances as high-performance lubricants, and there is even a replacement for use in extreme conditions—the oil of the jojoba plant. Plastic has long since made whalebone superfluous, and chemists can make ambergris substitutes.

In other words, there is no longer any justification for killing whales for raw materials.

The "Song of the Whale," a boat belonging to the International Fund for Animal Welfare (IFAW), carries out research on whales and investigates possible whale watching sites.

hundreds of dolphins every year, for example, supposedly to stop them from depleting fish stocks—even though it is not dolphins that cause the scarcity of fish but rather the excessive number of fishing boats. Now that commercial whaling is banned, whales are sometimes killed under the guise of "scientific research"—despite the fact that most scientists see no sense at all in such killing. They would much rather observe living whales.

In the Pacific alone, at least 100,000 dolphins die every year as a "side effect" of tuna fishing. They are caught in the nets and drown.

Lost or discarded fishing nets drifting in the ocean cause the death of an unknown number of whales and dolphins—and seabirds, turtles, and seals as well. Once these nets were made of hemp and decomposed quickly, but now they are made of synthetic materials and can last for decades. They are also "invisible" to the whales' echolocation systems. If the animals get tangled up in these

WHALE WATCHING is a new kind of "whaling" business where no blood is spilled. In 1996 there were nearly 70 countries that offered this kind of "eco-tourism"—including whaling countries like Japan, Norway, and Iceland. Six to seven million people have already participated in whale watches throughout the world.
To protect the whales from excessively curious boats and people, many countries have passed laws forbidding boats from surrounding the animals or from sailing too close to them.

> **Why are whales still becoming scarcer?**

Despite all these alternatives, these gentle giants are still being pursued and killed even today. Countries such as Japan and Norway still refuse to recognize the ban on whaling. The laws also provide for exceptions, for example, in the case of "aboriginal whaling"—whaling that is part of a traditional minority culture. Greenland, the Danish Faeroe Island, Alaska, Canada, and Russia make use of the quotas allowed under this ruling. Many species such as pilot whales, beluga whales, narwhals, and some dolphin species aren't included in the official ban and are still slaughtered by the thousands. Japanese fishermen kill

Researchers take pictures of every sperm whale that bares its flukes and then catalogue each according to its individual features.

"ghost nets" they drown in agony. Australia recently banned synthetic nets for this reason. Even if whaling were now stopped com-

Sperm whale mothers with calves don't dive as deep as fully-grown bulls. Off the shores of the Azores, there is a "nursery" for these toothed whales.

RAPIDLY INCREASING POLLUTION of the oceans with heavy metals, insecticides, and other environmental pollutants is becoming an ever-greater danger for whales. These pollutants accumulate in the body tissues of the whales. This reduces their resistance to disease and parasites and also lowers reproduction rates.

SEVERAL INTERNATIONAL ORGANIZATIONS are involved in protecting whales—for example, Greenpeace, the World Wide Fund for Nature (WWF), the International Fund for Animal Welfare (IFAW), and the Society for the Conservation of Marine Mammals (GSM). The work of such organizations has helped enact important laws protecting these animals.

pletely, however, it may well be too late to save some species from becoming extinct. So many male sperm whales were killed in the past in the northwest Pacific that, even today, many females don't become pregnant.

Through whaling and ocean pollution humankind has annihilated from 90 to 95 percent of the stocks of most species of whales used commercially, and several species such as the Atlantic gray whale, the Biscaya right whale, and the Korean gray whale are already extinct.

Despite frequent warnings in

What laws are there to protect whales?

the past, we have been slow to realize that the successes of the whaling industry may mean that one day there will be no

more whales. When the International Whaling Commission (IWC) was founded in 1946, it was not primarily because governments wanted to protect whales, but rather because they feared the whaling industry would collapse as the last of the whales disappeared. The commission sets quotas for the number of animals from each commercially hunted species that could be taken each year. Although the quotas were based solely on commercial considerations at first, in the meantime many non-whaling nations have joined the commission and have helped make the protection of animals one of the organization's goals. At present there is a ten-year "moratorium" (ban) on whaling. The IWC doesn't have any way to enforce its decisions, however. All the countries still interested in whaling have come up with various tricks and excuses in order to continue hunting whales.

More than 120 nations from around the globe have now ratified the CITES agreement—Convention on International Trade of Endangered Species of Fauna and Flora. This treaty bans both the importation and exportation of all whale products. This includes not only whale meat and oil, but also engraved sperm whale teeth—"scrimshaw"—which are still being offered for sale in the Azores and elsewhere.

Index